THE STORY OF THE
BOSTON

CREATIVE EDUCATION

Published by Creative Education
123 South Broad Street
Mankato, Minnesota 56001
Creative Education is an imprint of The Creative Company.

DESIGN AND PRODUCTION BY **EVANSDAY DESIGN**

PHOTOGRAPHS BY Getty Images (Brian Babineau / NBAE, Andrew D.
Bernstein / NBAE, Nathaniel S. Butler / NBAE, Louis Capozzola / NBAE,
Gary Dineen / NBAE, Focus on Sport, Greg Foster / NBAE, Walter
Looss Jr. / NBAE, George Marx / Retrofile, NBA Photos / NBAE, Joel
Sartore / National Geographic, Bill Smith / NBAE, Noren Trotman /
NBAE, Jerry Wachter / NBAE)

LIBRARY OF CONGRESS CATALOGING-IN-PUBLICATION DATA

LeBoutillier, Nate.
The story of the Boston Celtics / by Nate LeBoutillier.
p. cm. — (The NBA—a history of hoops)
Includes index.
ISBN-13: 978-1-58341-400-2
1. Boston Celtics (Basketball team)—History—
Juvenile literature. I. Title. II. Series.

GV885.52.B67L43 2006
796.323'64'0974461—dc22 2005050034

First edition

9 8 7 6 5 4 3 2 1

COVER PHOTO: *Paul Pierce*

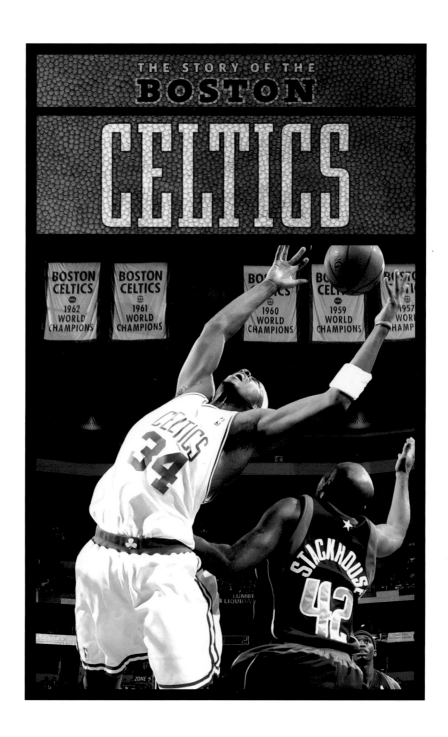

THE STORY OF THE
BOSTON
CELTICS

NATE LeBOUTILLIER

CREATIVE ♠ EDUCATION

Have the Boston Celtics

ALWAYS HAD SOME LUCKY CHARM? MAYBE IT WAS

THEIR CIGAR-SMOKING COACH, RED AUERBACH. MAYBE

IT WAS THEIR HEADY LITTLE POINT GUARD IN THE '50S,

BOB COUSY, OR THEIR CLASSY CENTER OF THE '60S,

BILL RUSSELL. MAYBE IT WAS THEIR OLD, SWAYING

BUILDING, THE BOSTON GARDEN, WITH ITS WARM

TEMPERATURE, CRAZY FANS, AND RICKETY PARQUET

PLAYING FLOOR. MAYBE IT WAS THEIR '80S HERO, LARRY

BIRD. OR MAYBE, JUST MAYBE, IT HAS TO DO WITH THE

LUCK OF THE IRISH AND THE TEAM'S LOGO, WHICH

DEPICTS A CHUBBY, WINKING LEPRECHAUN.

BOSTON CELTICS
Boston Massachusetts

THE CELTICS ARE BORN

BOSTON, MASSACHUSETTS, IS A CITY RICH WITH history. Puritans seeking to escape religious persecution in Europe settled there in 1630. The nation's first public school was founded in Boston in 1635, and Alexander Graham Bell invented the telephone there in 1876. Today, Boston is home to some of the nation's finest industries, universities, and museums.

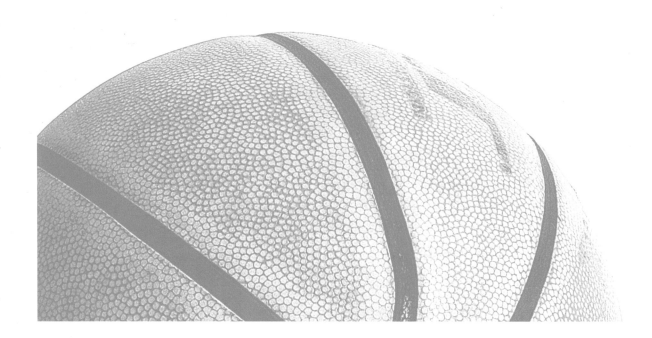

9

Red Auerbach spent more than 50 years with the Celtics, serving as coach, general manager, and president

10

As flashy as he was smart, point guard Bob Cousy was an NBA All-Star for 13 seasons in a row

One of the other points of pride among Boston's citizens is the city's National Basketball Association (NBA) team. Born in 1946, the Boston Celtics were named in honor of the city's large Irish population, and from the beginning, they captured the hearts of Bostonians.

The Celtics tipped off their first season in 1946 playing in an 11-team league called the Basketball Association of America (BAA). After three seasons, the BAA's teams merged to form the NBA. The Celtics' first four seasons were losing ones, but in 1950, the team hired a brash young coach by the name of Arnold "Red" Auerbach. Auerbach quickly taught the Celtics that he would not tolerate losing, and that winning could be achieved only through teamwork.

Auerbach soon reshaped his roster, adding young talents such as point guard Bob Cousy, shooting guard Bill Sharman, and forward Chuck Cooper. Of these players, Cousy made the biggest impact. The flashy, 6-foot-1 spitfire could control the ball like it had a handle on it, and his sleight-of-hand passes often fooled opponents as well as his own teammates, who occasionally were surprised to have a ball bounce off their foreheads. "Cousy was the catalyst for our team," said Auerbach. "He drove the guys to play their best."

VOICE OF THE CELTICS

From 1953 to 1990, when Celtics games were broadcast on television, many fans in the Boston area would turn down the sound on their TV sets and flick on their radios. They would then sit back and listen to the game called by fellow Celtics fan Johnny Most, the team's radio announcer. Early on, Most made his mark by clearly rooting for the Celtics in his broadcasts—and occasionally making villains of opponents or referees. Most often traveled and roomed with players, becoming lifelong friends with many. "He hated phonies, and he wasn't going to be one," said Most's son, Jamie. "He was going to root for his team, and he didn't care if people called him a 'homer.' He stayed true to himself, and in his mind that was the most important thing."

RUSSELL SIGNS ON

FROM 1950 TO 1956, THE CELTICS MADE THE PLAYOFFS every year. But Auerbach wanted a championship. In the 1956 NBA Draft, the Celtics traded for the right to draft an athletic center from the University of San Francisco by the name of Bill Russell. The 6-foot-9 and 220-pound rookie prowled the lane aggressively, blocking shots and pulling down rebounds at a remarkable pace. "We needed a big defender in order to get over the top," said Auerbach.

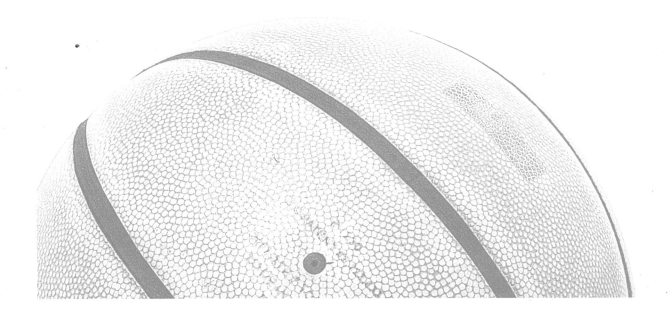

CELTICS

13

Many people consider 1950s and '60s great Bill Russell the best defensive player in the history of the NBA

Guard K.C. Jones served in the Army for two years, then helped the Celtics win eight NBA championships

Behind their big man, the 1956–57 Celtics went 44–28 and tore through the playoffs to meet the St. Louis Hawks in the NBA Finals. After six hard-fought games, the series was deadlocked. The deciding Game 7 was a classic struggle. The Celtics and Hawks battled through two overtimes before Boston finally pulled out a 125–123 victory to claim its first NBA championship, and Auerbach predicted it was only the beginning.

Coach Auerbach proved to be a prophet as the Celtics rolled to an incredible nine world championships in the next 10 years. With Russell and Cousy providing the leadership, potent talents such as guards K.C. Jones and Sam Jones and forwards Tom Heinsohn and Tom "Satch" Sanders delivered much of the team's punch.

During the Celtics' charmed run, Russell averaged more than 16 points, 23 rebounds, and 4 assists per game. He also won the NBA's Most Valuable Player (MVP) award five times with a devotion to winning and teamwork that set him apart. "Russell was the greatest competitor I ever coached," said Auerbach.

After Boston's 1965–66 championship season, Auerbach retired from coaching and moved to the front office. To replace him, the Celtics turned to Russell, who accepted the dual role of player-coach and became the first African-American coach in NBA history. During Russell's three years at the helm, the Celtics won two more world championships, including one in 1968–69, Russell's final season as a Celtics player and coach.

PLAYING "CELTICS BASKETBALL"

BOSTON'S FIRST SEASON AFTER RUSSELL'S RETIREMENT
yielded a 34–48 record. All at once, the Celtics' magic
seemed to disappear. Many experts thought the Celtics
were in for a long period of rebuilding under new coach
Tom Heinsohn. The experts were wrong.

By the 1970–71 season, talented players such as brawny
center Dave Cowens and sweet-shooting guard Jo Jo
White had been added to a lineup that already fea-
tured do-it-all forward John Havlicek. The Celtics rose

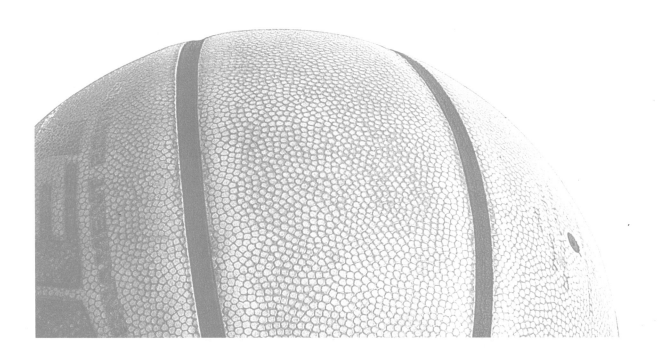

CELTICS

Although not blessed with great athletic ability, Dave Cowens excelled thanks to his tireless work ethic

17

18

A superb all-around talent, guard Jo Jo White averaged 18 points a game during his 10-year Boston career

quickly, and by 1973, the team was once again among the league's elite. "We play Celtics basketball," explained Havlicek. "We work hard every night, and we don't care who gets the glory. It's all about the team."

In 1973–74, the Celtics went 56–26. Suddenly, Boston found itself facing the Milwaukee Bucks for the NBA championship. The Bucks were led by the league's most dominant big man, Kareem Abdul-Jabbar, and after six games, the series stood tied. In Game 7, Cowens erupted for 28 points to lead the Celtics to a 102–87 victory and the franchise's 12th NBA title.

In 1976, Boston rose to championship heights once more, winning a thrilling NBA Finals series against the Phoenix Suns. The 35-year-old Havlicek, though hobbled by a leg injury, led the charge. Two years later, the 13-time All-Star retired. "Nobody ever played this game harder than Havlicek," said Celtics forward Don Nelson. "He was as tough as they come."

HAVLICEH STOLE THE BALL!

Celtics forward John Havlicek scored 26,395 career points—the most in team history—but he sealed his legend with a defensive play. With only five seconds remaining in Game 7 of the 1965 Eastern Conference Finals and his team clinging to a 110–109 lead, Havlicek pulled off the most famed play in franchise history. The Philadelphia 76ers had one last shot, and 76ers guard Hal Greer was taking the ball out from under the basket. Celtics announcer Johnny Most's crackling words describing the action became nearly as famous as the play itself: *Greer is putting the ball into play. He gets it out deep…Havlicek steals it. Over to Sam Jones. Havlicek stole the ball! It's all over! Johnny Havlicek stole the ball!* The Celtics won the game and eventually captured the 1965 NBA crown.

BIRD SENDS CELTICS SOARING

IN THE 1979 NBA DRAFT, BOSTON SELECTED FORWARD Larry Bird from Indiana State University. From his puffy hair to his spotty mustache to his extra-pale complexion, the long-limbed Bird looked awkward—that is, until he released his jump shot. A high-arcing thing of beauty, Bird's shot almost always found the net when his team needed it most. Cleveland Cavaliers public address announcer Howie Chizek, whose team was just one of Bird's many repeat victims, once said, "Larry Bird just throws the ball in the air and God moves the basket underneath it."

21

SPALDING

Larry Bird's flawless shooting form earned him three NBA MVP awards and the nickname "Larry Legend"

Big center Robert "Chief" Parish set an NBA record for most defensive rebounds (10,117) in a career

The Celtics had also engineered some shrewd trades, acquiring point guard Nate "Tiny" Archibald in 1978 and center Robert "Chief" Parish in 1980 to complement Bird and forward Cedric "Cornbread" Maxwell. In the 1980 Draft, the Celtics struck gold yet again, acquiring 6-foot-11 power forward Kevin McHale.

In 1980–81, the recharged Celtics barreled to a 62–20 mark. Boston then stormed to the NBA Finals, where its swarm of stars overwhelmed the scrappy Houston Rockets in six games to make Boston a champion once more. Two seasons later, under new coach K.C. Jones, the Celtics beat their archrivals, the Los Angeles Lakers, for another championship. As Bird famously dueled with the Lakers' star guard, Magic Johnson, the NBA's popularity rose to an all-time high.

Bird and the Celtics lost only one game at home during a scintillating 1985–86 season and claimed yet another NBA championship, dispatching the Houston Rockets in the NBA Finals. Joining Bird, McHale, and Parish in the starting lineup were guards Dennis Johnson and Danny Ainge, with center Bill Walton as Boston's top bench player. "This Celtics team," wrote journalist Jack McCallum, "can take its place alongside any that has gone before."

"Larry Legend," as the Celtics' faithful called the star forward, led Boston's charge until 1992, when chronic back problems forced him to retire. Bird finished with career averages of 24 points, 10 rebounds, and 6 assists per game—numbers that gained him entry into the Hall of Fame.

KICK FROM FRENCH LICK

Raised in the small Indiana town of French Lick (population approximately 2,000), Larry Bird was no surefire guarantee to "make it big." He eventually went on to find fame and fortune with the Boston Celtics, but there was a time when Bird almost settled for a life as... a garbage man? In 1975, Bird dropped out of college at Indiana University and moved back home, where he took up a job with the French Lick Street Department. "We picked up trash once a week," recalled Bird years later. "We were out mowing grass in the summer, and in the winter we took care of snow removal. We fixed roads. I was working outside and loving every minute of it." Thankfully for the Celtics, Bird returned to college and basketball the next year.

25

Kevin McHale's assortment of almost unstoppable low-post moves earned him a place in the Hall of Fame

CELTICS MYSTIQUE TAKES A HIT

IN THE LATE 1980S, BOSTON'S FORTUNES BEGAN TO change. In 1986, the Celtics drafted a 21-year-old stand-out forward named Len Bias, but, tragically, he died shortly after the draft as a result of a drug overdose. "Lenny Bias was a phenomenal talent," said Celtics team president Red Auerbach. "He could do it all."

CELTICS

27

A quiet leader, Reggie Lewis played six strong seasons before his tragic death in 1993 at the age of 27

28

Paul Pierce was a standout at college powerhouse Kansas before becoming the Celtics' latest hero

The next year, Boston spent its top draft pick on Reggie Lewis, a multital-ented forward from Boston's own Northeastern University. The 6-foot-8 Lewis instantly brought youthful energy to Boston's lineup, and by 1992, he was an All-Star and the rightful heir to Bird's throne as the leader of the Celtics. But in July 1993, he died of a heart attack. The twin tragedies deprived the Celtics of the two stars they had counted on to lead the team into the post-Bird era.

The Celtics suffered through a number of losing seasons in the 1990s. Looking to rebuild, Boston hired successful college coach Rick Pitino as its new head coach and team president in 1997. But Pitino would never see the Celtics to a winning record. Young players such as forwards Antoine Walker and Paul Pierce and center Vitaly Potapenko showed flashes of brilliance but also struggled while adjusting to the pro game. In 2001, Jim O'Brien replaced Pitino and coached the Celtics to their first winning re-cord (49–33) since the 1992–93 season.

Pierce and Walker rose to the ranks of team co-captains early in the 21st century, each averaging more than 20 points per game for three straight

TWIN TRAGEDIES

June 17, 1986, seemed to be the day that the "Celtic Mystique" ran out. Just 12 days earlier, the Celtics had won the NBA championship. Just two days earlier, the team had made University of Maryland forward Len Bias, perhaps the most talented collegiate player available, the second overall pick in the NBA Draft. But on June 17, Bias died of a cocaine overdose. "It hurt our sport," said famous Duke University coach Mike Krzyzewski. "Above and beyond the loss of life, we never got to see one of those truly great ones become great." In July 1993, tragedy again struck the Celtics when six-year veteran and team captain Reggie Lewis collapsed and died while shooting baskets with a friend. The tragedies seemed to hurt the Celtics for years afterwards.

seasons. Walker was traded to the Atlanta Hawks in 2003, but Pierce helped carry the Celtics to the 2004 playoffs, where they lost to the Indiana Pacers in the first round.

In 2004–05, under new coach Doc Rivers, the Celtics won the Atlantic Division but lost to the Pacers again in the playoffs. Just weeks later, the team selected 19-year-old forward Gerald Green in the 2005 NBA Draft. Celtics fans hoped Green would team with Boston's young draft picks of 2004—forward Al Jefferson and guard Delonte West—to lead Boston back to greatness. "These are guys," said Celtics director of basketball operations Danny Ainge, "that anyone in the league would kill to have."

The Boston Celtics are among the NBA's proudest franchise, with 16 championship banners flapping from their rafters. From Cousy to Russell to Havlicek to Bird, the Celtics have always seemed able to find the next great player just as the previous star left the NBA stage. Boston is today looking for that player to help add to the Celtics' mystique. A little bit of Irish luck never hurt, either.

DEE BROWN PUMPS IT UP

For eight seasons during the 1990s, Dee Brown was a solid guard on solid, if unspectacular, Celtics teams. He was a decent passer, scorer, and defender. Although Brown was never a superstar, he enjoyed one star moment. During the 1991 NBA All-Star Game weekend, the 6-foot-1 rookie participated in the Slam Dunk Contest. After making it to the final round, Brown stared down at his shoes trying to think of an idea. That was it—the shoes! Wearing Reebok Pumps, the first shoes made that inflated like a basketball to provide a snug fit, Brown pumped up his shoes as the delighted crowd looked on. He then raced to the basket, leaped, covered his eyes with his right arm, and threw down a "no-look" slam with his left hand that won the competition.

31

A midseason trade in 2005–06 put forward Wally Szczerbiak, one of the NBA's best shooters, in Celtics green